**YOU
CAN
DO IT.**

summersdale

YOU CAN DO IT

An Hachette UK Company
www.hachette.co.uk

Summersdale Publishers Ltd
Part of Octopus Publishing Group Limited
Carmelite House
50 Victoria Embankment
LONDON
EC4Y 0DZ
UK

www.summersdale.com

Printed and bound in the Czech Republic

ISBN: 978-1-78685-944-0

Substantial discounts on bulk quantities of Summersdale books are available to corporations, professional associations and other organisations. For details contact general enquiries: telephone: +44 (0) 1243 771107 or email: enquiries@summersdale.com.

**To**...................................

**From**...............................

If you think
you can do
it, you can.

**John Burroughs**

The brave man is not he who does not feel afraid, but he who conquers that fear.

**Nelson Mandela**

Your attitude is like a
box of crayons that
colour your world.

**Allen Klein**

**YOU HAVE TO BE UNIQUE AND DIFFERENT AND SHINE IN YOUR OWN WAY.**

Lady Gaga

Fear, to a great extent,
is born of a story we
tell ourselves.

**Cheryl Strayed**

Life is a pure flame,
and we live by an
invisible sun within us.

**Thomas Browne**

Don't let the fear
of falling keep you
from climbing up.

**Constance Chuks Friday**

Wherever you go,
no matter what the
weather, always bring
your own sunshine.

Anthony J. D'Angelo

ALWAYS
AIM TO BE
A LITTLE BIT
BETTER THAN
YOU WERE
YESTERDAY.

It takes courage to
grow up and become
who you really are.

E. E. Cummings

# THE SECRET OF GETTING AHEAD IS GETTING STARTED.

**Mark Twain**

The brave man is not
he who does not feel
afraid, but he who
conquers that fear.

**Nelson Mandela**

You are not stuck
where you are unless
you decide to be.

**Wayne W. Dyer**

# *Live your own life and follow your own star.*

**Wilferd Peterson**

There is always room at the top.

**Daniel Webster**

OPTIMISM IS
THE FAITH
THAT LEADS TO
ACHIEVEMENT.
NOTHING CAN BE
DONE WITHOUT
HOPE AND
CONFIDENCE.

**Helen Keller**

*To accomplish great things, we must not only act, but also dream; not only plan, but also believe.*

Anatole France

# DOUBT WHOM YOU WILL, BUT NEVER YOURSELF.

**Christian Nestell Bovee**

# YOUR
# PERSONALITY

# LIGHTS UP
# THE WHOLE
# ROOM.

You cannot change what you are, only what you do.

**Philip Pullman**

If you want to have
the time of your life,
change how you use
the time in your life.

**Tim Fargo**

# Fortune favours the prepared mind.

**Louis Pasteur**

The man who removes
a mountain begins
by carrying away
small stones.

**Chinese proverb**

**YOU MUST LEARN A NEW WAY TO THINK** BEFORE YOU CAN MASTER A NEW WAY TO BE.

**Marianne Williamson**

You never know when
that next obstacle is
going to be the last one.

**Chuck Norris**

Always do what you
are afraid to do.

Ralph Waldo Emerson

**MAKE BOLD CHOICES AND MAKE MISTAKES. IT'S ALL THOSE THINGS THAT ADD UP TO THE PERSON YOU BECOME.**

Angelina Jolie

Always be a first-rate
version of yourself,
instead of a second-rate
version of somebody else.

**Judy Garland**

Human potential is the
only limitless resource
we have in this world.

**Carly Fiorina**

**WRITE
YOUR OWN
DESTINY.**

If you think you are too small to make a difference, try sleeping with a mosquito.

**Dalai Lama**

# THE MOST COURAGEOUS ACT IS STILL TO THINK FOR YOURSELF.

Coco Chanel

*Luck is not as random as you think. Before that lottery ticket won the jackpot, someone had to buy it.*

**Vera Nazarian**

Have patience with
all things, but first of
all with yourself.

**Francis de Sales**

What progress, you ask, have I made? I have begun to be a friend to myself.

Hecato

TO LOVE
YOURSELF RIGHT
NOW, JUST AS
YOU ARE, IS TO
GIVE YOURSELF
HEAVEN.

**Alan Cohen**

Expect problems and
eat them for breakfast.

**Alfred A. Montapert**

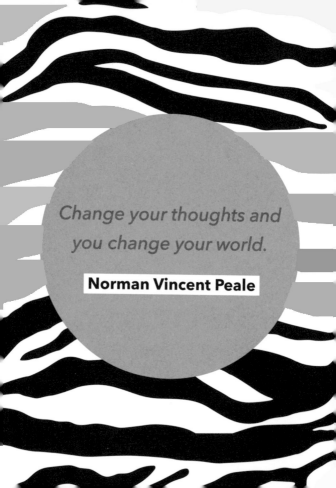

*Change your thoughts and you change your world.*

**Norman Vincent Peale**

Look at everything
as though you were
seeing it for the first
time or the last time.

**Betty Smith**

Life is a helluva lot
more fun if you say
yes rather than no.

**Richard Branson**

Find out who you are
and do it on purpose.

**Dolly Parton**

# BELIEVE
# AND
# ACHIEVE!

Always act like
you're wearing an
invisible crown.

Anonymous

**FAILURES
ARE LIKE
SKINNED KNEES:
PAINFUL BUT
SUPERFICIAL.**

H. Ross Perot

It is often in the darkest skies that we see the brightest stars.

**Richard Paul Evans**

People who can change
and change again
are so much more
reliable and happier
than those who can't.

**Stephen Fry**

# Be bold or italic.

## Never just regular.

**Anonymous**

Live your life, sing
your song. Not full
of expectations.
Not for the ovations.
But for the joy of it.

**Rasheed Ogunlaru**

# AMBITION IS THE PATH TO SUCCESS. PERSISTENCE IS THE VEHICLE YOU ARRIVE IN.

**Bill Bradley**

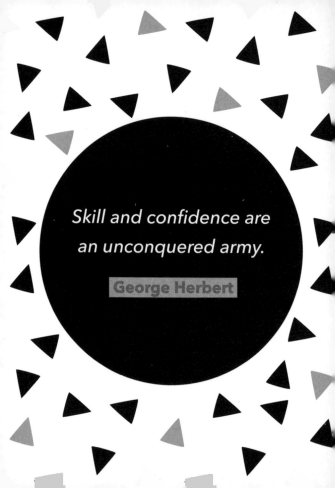

*Skill and confidence are an unconquered army.*

George Herbert

Don't be afraid to speak up for yourself. Keep fighting for your dreams!

**Gabby Douglas**

# THE ONLY REAL LIMIT

**IS YOUR
IMAGINATION.**

If you're going through
hell, keep going.

**Anonymous**

When you're true to
who you are, amazing
things happen.

**Deborah Norville**

**Watch the stars, and see yourself running with them.**

Marcus Aurelius

Motivation is what gets you started. Habit is what keeps you going.

**Jim Ryun**

# NOTHING IS A WASTE OF TIME IF YOU USE THE EXPERIENCE WISELY.

**Auguste Rodin**

If there is a good will,
there is great way.

**William Shakespeare**

# THE PAST CANNOT BE CHANGED. THE FUTURE IS YET IN YOUR POWER.

**Mary Pickford**

*Think big thoughts but relish small pleasures.*

**H. Jackson Brown Jr**

Be brave enough to live creatively… what you discover will be wonderful. What you discover will be yourself.

**Alan Alda**

Begin, be bold and venture to be wise.

**Horace**

# EMBRACE
# THE
# UNKNOWN.

Thoughts become
things… choose
the good ones!

**Mike Dooley**

The future depends on
what you do today.

**Mahatma Gandhi**

You are perfectly cast
in your life. I can't
imagine anyone but you
in the role. Go play.

**Lin-Manuel Miranda**

Follow your inner moonlight; don't hide the madness.

**Allen Ginsberg**

Life is what you make it. Always has been, always will be.

**Eleanor Roosevelt**

The greatest danger
in life is not taking
the adventure.

**Brian Blessed**

Scared is what you're feeling. Brave is what you're doing.

**Emma Donoghue**

# THERE'S NOTHING MORE INTOXICATING THAN DOING BIG, BOLD THINGS.

**Jason Kilar**

Those who wish to sing
always find a song.

**Swedish proverb**

# BE STRONG,
# BE FEARLESS,
# BE BEAUTIFUL.

**Misty Copeland**

It always seems
impossible until
it's done.

**Nelson Mandela**

# DON'T COUNT THE **DAYS**: MAKE THE **DAYS COUNT!**

Be brave enough to
be your true self.

**Queen Latifah**

Be yourself. The world
worships the original.

**Ingrid Bergman**

# YOU MISS 100% OF THE SHOTS YOU DON'T TAKE.

**Wayne Gretzky**

It is only by being bold that you get anywhere.

**Richard Branson**

*You cannot find peace
by avoiding life.*

**Michael Cunningham**

Commitment leads to action. Action brings your dream closer.

**Marcia Wieder**

# LIFE SHRINKS
# OR EXPANDS IN
# PROPORTION TO
# ONE'S COURAGE.

**Anaïs Nin**

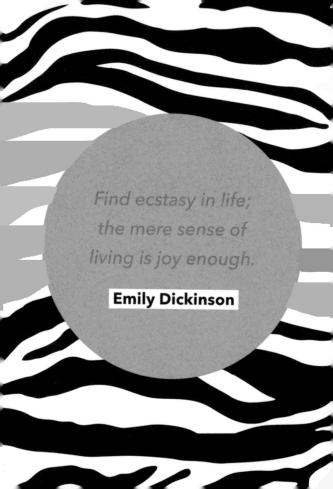

Find ecstasy in life;
the mere sense of
living is joy enough.

**Emily Dickinson**

It does not matter how slowly you go as long as you do not stop.

**Confucius**

# PLAY THE GAME OF LIFE WITH

# A BOLD SPIRIT AND AN OPEN HEART.

I always believe
that the sky is the
beginning of the limit.

**MC Hammer**

Why not just live in the moment, especially if it has a good beat?

Goldie Hawn

# Keep your eyes on the stars, and your feet on the ground.

**Theodore Roosevelt**

Joy is of the will
which labours, which
overcomes obstacles,
which knows triumph.

**W. B. Yeats**

Believe in yourself. Pick a path that you, deep down in your soul, won't be ashamed of.

Hiromu Arakawa

The dreamers are the saviours of the world.

**James Allen**

# I COULDN'T FIND THE SPORTS CAR OF MY DREAMS, SO I BUILT IT MYSELF.

**Ferdinand Porsche**

*Dare to love yourself as if you were a rainbow with gold at both ends.*

**Aberjhani**

Freedom lies in being bold.

**Robert Frost**

# BE NOT AFRAID OF GOING SLOWLY; BE AFRAID ONLY OF STANDING STILL.

**Chinese proverb**

# NOW IS THE BEST TIME TO START.

You are magnificent
beyond measure, perfect
in your imperfections,
and wonderfully made.

**Abiola Abrams**

There's no one alive
who is you-er than you.

**Dr Seuss**

Wherever you are
– be all there.

**Jim Elliot**

Unfold your own myth.

Rumi

*Success doesn't come to you; you go to it.*

T. Scott McLeod

Don't let what you
cannot do interfere
with what you can do.

**John Wooden**

Trust yourself. You
know more than
you think you do.

**Benjamin Spock**

# A JOURNEY OF A THOUSAND MILES BEGINS WITH A SINGLE STEP.

**Lao Tzu**

Be faithful to that
which exists nowhere
but in yourself.

**André Gide**

Don't waste your energy trying to change opinions... do your thing, and don't care if they like it.

**Tina Fey**

# FOLLOW YOUR DREAMS. THEY KNOW THE WAY.

**Kobi Yamada**

**FIND YOUR SONG AND SING IT.**

I believe that if one always looked at the skies, one would end up with wings.

**Gustave Flaubert**

Nothing can dim the light
that shines from within.

**Maya Angelou**

A wise man will make
more opportunities
than he finds.

**Francis Bacon**

At the end of the day, let there be no excuses, no explanations, no regrets.

**Steve Maraboli**

*In my moments of doubt I've told myself firmly: if not me, who? If not now, when?*

**Emma Watson**

# YOUR BIG OPPORTUNITY MAY BE RIGHT WHERE YOU ARE NOW.

Napoleon Hill

You are the only
person on earth who
can use your ability.

**Zig Ziglar**

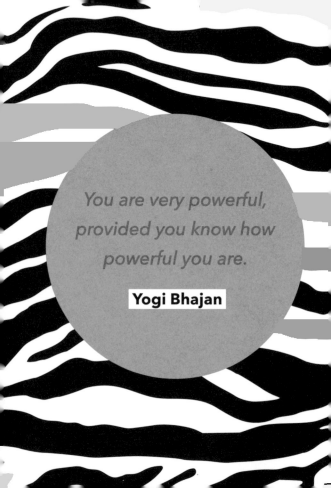

You are very powerful,
provided you know how
powerful you are.

**Yogi Bhajan**

No one can make you
feel inferior without
your consent.

**Eleanor Roosevelt**

# THOSE
# WHO DON'T
# BELIEVE
# IN MAGIC

# WILL NEVER
# FIND IT.

Courage is found in
unlikely places.

**J. R. R. Tolkien**

Think like a queen.
A queen is not afraid
to fail. Failure is
another stepping
stone to greatness.

**Oprah Winfrey**

# This life is what you make it.

**Marilyn Monroe**

A strong, positive
self-image is the best
possible preparation
for success.

**Joyce Brothers**

# THE SWEETEST PLEASURES ARE THOSE WHICH ARE HARDEST TO BE WON.

**Giacomo Casanova**

The first step is you have
to say that you can.

**Will Smith**

Aim high! The future
you see, is the person
you will be.

**Jim Cathcart**

*Put your future in good hands – your own.*

**Mark Victor Hansen**

With realisation of
one's own potential
and self-confidence in
one's ability, one can
build a better world.

**Dalai Lama**

# YOU HAVE TO EXPECT THINGS OF YOURSELF BEFORE YOU CAN DO THEM.

**Michael Jordan**

**KEEP ASKING UNTIL YOU GET THE ANSWER.**

Always be yourself… do not go out and look for a successful personality and try to duplicate it.

Bruce Lee

If you can dream it,
you can do it.

Tom Fitzgerald

WE MUST NOT ALLOW OTHER PEOPLE'S LIMITED PERCEPTIONS TO DEFINE US.

Virginia Satir

Set your goals high,
and don't stop till
you get there.

**Bo Jackson**

# Well done is better than well said.

**Benjamin Franklin**

Most people fail in life not because they aim too high and miss, but because they aim too low and hit.

**Les Brown**

It is not wrong to be
different. Sometimes it is
hard, but it is not wrong.

**Elizabeth Moon**

*Self-confidence and self-courage are your greatest strengths.*

**Lailah Gifty Akita**

**DON'T GIVE IN TO YOUR FEARS...** IF YOU DO, YOU WON'T BE ABLE TO TALK TO YOUR HEART.

**Paulo Coelho**

Don't be a blueprint.
Be an original.

**Roy Acuff**

Plunge boldly into the
thick of life, and seize
it where you will.

Johann Wolfgang von Goethe

# HAVE CONFIDENCE IN YOUR DECISIONS.

Your aspirations are
your possibilities.

**Samuel Johnson**

Don't let them tame you.

Isadora Duncan

# EVERYTHING IS PHENOMENAL; EVERYTHING IS INCREDIBLE; NEVER TREAT LIFE CASUALLY.

Abraham Joshua Heschel

Your life is a book;
make it a bestseller.

**Shanon Grey**

*Don't live down
to expectations.
Go out there and do
something remarkable.*

**Wendy Wasserstein**

To be bold is to be wise enough to realise that fear is the energy that fuels action.

Craig D. Lounsbrough

# IT IS THE CHIEFEST POINT OF HAPPINESS

## THAT A MAN IS WILLING TO BE WHAT HE IS.

**Desiderius Erasmus**

# FALL SEVEN TIMES AND STAND UP EIGHT.

Japanese proverb

Those who matter don't mind, and those who mind don't matter.

**Bernard Baruch**

# TAKE THE FIRST STEP TO SUCCESS.

# YOU CAN
# DO IT!

If you're interested in finding out more about our books, find us on Facebook at **Summersdale Publishers** and follow us on Twitter at @Summersdale.

# www.summersdale.com

### Image credits

pp.9, 42, 88, 122 © yellowpixel/Shutterstock.com
pp.20, 54, 133 © Alex Landa/Shutterstock.com
pp.26, 60, 94, 128, 160 © Alex Kednert/Shutterstock.com
pp.30, 77, 110, 156 © Oxy_gen/Shutterstock.com
pp.17, 51, 85, 119, 153 © Brian Goff/Shutterstock.com